Woodmill High School Library

T02540

2540
205.8

LIFE FILES

This book is to be returned on or before
the last date stamped below.

27 OCT 2000

KT-433-552

RACISM

JAGDISH GUNDARA & ROGER HEWITT

EVANS BROTHERS LIMITED

2540
305.8

Evans Brothers LImited
2A Portman Mansions
Chiltern Street
London W1M 1LE

©Evans Brothers Limited 1999

All rights reserved. No part of this publication may be
reproduced, stored in a retrieval system or transmitted
in any form or by any means, electronic, mechanical,
photocopying, recording or otherwise, without prior
permission of Evans Brothers Limited.

First published 1999

British Library Cataloguing in Publication Data.

Gundara, Jagdish
  Racism. - (Life Files)
  1.Racism - Juvenile literature
  I.Title II.Hewitt, Roger
  305.8[J]

ISBN 0 237 51654 3 (paperback)

ACKNOWLEDGEMENTS

Editorial: Su Swallow
Design: Tinstar Design
Production: Jenny Mulvanny

For permission to reproduce copyright material
the Author and Publishers gratefully acknowledge
the following: **page 6** Danny Lyon/Magnum Photos
page 9 Bernard Gerard/ The Hutchison Library **page
10** Laguna Design/Science Photo Library **page 12**
mckenzie heritage picture archive **page 14** Mary
Evans Picture Library **page 15** Glyn Kirk/Action Plus
page 16 Corbis-Bettman **page 18** Crispin Hughes/The
Hutchison Picture Library **page 20** Paul Chesley/Tony
Stone **page 21** Mary Evans Picture Library **page 22**
AKG **page 25** John Birdsall Photography **page 27**
Jeni Mckenzie/mckenzie heritage picture archive
page 28 Danny Lyon/ Magnum Photos **page 29**
Corbis-Bettmann **page 31** Serge Attal/ Image Bank
page 32 S Franklin/Magnum **page 34** Corbis-
Bettmann **page 35** Steve McCurry/Magnum **page 36**
Philip Wolmuth/Hutchison Library **page 39** Agence
France Presse/Corbis-Bettmann **page 41** Nigel
Dickinson/Getty Images **page 42** Chris Steele-
Perkins/Magnum **page 43** David Alan Harvey/
Magnum **page 45** John Birdsall Photography **page
46** P Moszynski/The Hutchison Library **page 47**
John Birdsall Photography **page 48** Abbas/
Magnum **page 51** Eli Reed/Magnum Photos **page 52**
Lynn Goldsmith/Corbis **page 55** Bruce Davidson/
Magnum **page 56** Ingrid Hudson/The Hutchison
Picture Library **page 57** Jeni Mckenzie/mckenzie
heritage picture archive

CONTENTS

INTRODUCTION

Wherever people are harassed because of the colour of their skin, or cannot get jobs, receive as good an education as others, or get the same legal representation because of their 'racial' or ethnic group, then racism is at work.

> **Racism can mean a belief in the superiority of a particular race, or prejudice based on this belief. It can mean antagonism towards, or discrimination against, other races. It can also refer to the theory that human abilities are determined by race.**

Racism today is very much bound up with racism in the past, when it took some very cruel forms. The sufferings of the Jews throughout history and particularly during the Holocaust under the Nazis, the long history of slavery and the oppression of black people in the United States, the Caribbean and South America, and the cruelties of the apartheid system in South Africa until very recently, are some of the best known examples of racism in modern history.

A café in Georgia, Atlanta, USA. Even as late as the 1960s, black Americans, particularly in the southern states, were kept separate from white people in most public places.

History follows people into the world today because even when a people are no longer persecuted, the pain lives on in memories and in what happens as a consequence of persecution. Black people whose ancestors suffered slavery are still living with the effects of slavery. Whole social groups cannot go from slavery to economic prosperity overnight, even if some individuals are able to. Most still live with the long struggle for education, jobs, health and legal and social status, despite the achievements of the African-American Civil Rights Movement.

There are many other groups in the world who have also suffered greatly from racism. For example, a 1996 report on education in the Czech Republic cites attacks by skinheads on Romani (gypsy) children, and on foreign students, singled out for their dark skin. In one incident, witnesses reported that when the police arrived, their first question to 'white' students was: "Are these gypsies bothering you?"

A report called 'Inside Racist Europe', by the Institute of Race Relations, describes other examples of apparent racism:

> " At Lisbon airport, the national airline of Portugal, TAP, has since October 1991 photocopied the passports of all non-white passengers travelling to the UK, Germany, the US and Canada, since, a spokesman said, they were all 'potential clandestine immigrants'. "

> " In Vienna throughout 1992 refugee hostels were firebombed. After an attack on one centre in September the mayors of Salzburg and Vienna did not condemn the violence but announced instead that they would take in no more refugees. "

This book looks at racism in the world today. In doing so it will also make many references to the history of racism across the globe and to many different groups. This book is also about how people all over the world have fought racism and continue to fight it.

But in fighting racism many questions arise. Is someone who feels uncomfortable in the presence of people from a different country to be called a 'racist'? Is that person as racist as someone who harasses his ethnic-minority neighbours in an attempt to get them to move? Is religious persecution always different from racial persecution or do the two sometimes overlap? Are anti-Irish jokes in England racist?

These are just some of the many questions that this book opens up for discussion. There may be no right or wrong answers but the issues deserve to be considered in informed, thoughtful ways.

WHAT IS RACISM?

Racism has been defined as the belief that some of the 'races of mankind' are superior to others. The 'superior races' were seen as more intelligent, more civilised, more creative, more capable of scientific invention and even, more moral - in other words, better human beings. People have used this idea of 'higher races' and 'lower races' to justify slavery, forced transportation, economic exploitation and even genocide - the killing of hundreds and thousands of men, women and children because they were said to be members of certain 'races' and should be 'eliminated'.

Not only has this cruelty inflicted untold human suffering over the centuries, the very thing it has been based on - the idea that there are different races in the sense of types or grades - is now known by genetic science to be untrue. There are no such things as distinct races of mankind. Within the human form the range of differences between individuals is very large indeed, and the clustering of features such as skin colour and hair type - which are often taken to be the signs of 'racial' difference - are just a tiny part of the possible range of DNA variation of

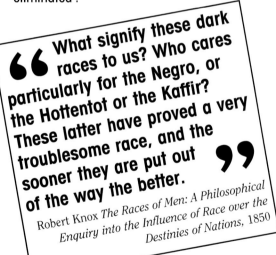

> " What signify these dark races to us? Who cares particularly for the Negro, or the Hottentot or the Kaffir? These latter have proved a very troublesome race, and the sooner they are put out of the way the better. "
>
> Robert Knox *The Races of Men: A Philosophical Enquiry into the Influence of Race over the Destinies of Nations*, 1850

Racism starts when people begin to perceive differences between themselves and others. At what age do children start to be aware of such differences?

which we are made up. People with similar skin colour, for example, and alike in that way, are also unalike in so many other ways that to say they are members of a distinct 'race' makes little more sense than to say that people who can roll their tongues longways and those who can't, are two distinct 'races'!

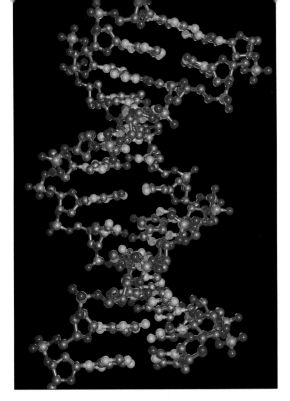

A computer image of a DNA molecule. As geneticists have learnt more about human variation, the old concept of race is rapidly disappearing.

> **Hundreds of different genes... have been mapped...The picture which emerges is quite different from that supported by those who believe that the human species is divided into distinct races distinguished by skin colour. In fact the trends in skin colour are not accompanied by those in other genes...When gene geography is used to look at overall patterns of variation it seems that people from different parts of the world do not differ much on average. Colour does not say much about what lies under the skin.**
>
> Steve Jones, Professor of Genetics, *The Language of Genes*, 1993

> **Some have thought fit to employ 'races' for four or five divisions according to regions of origin or complexion. I see no reason for employing this term... Complexions run into each other and they are but different shades of the same great picture which extends through all ages and all parts of the Earth.**
>
> J. G. Herder, 18th-century German philosopher

Question

Some people say, 'There's only one race - the human race.' What does this mean? Do you agree?

Since science opened the door to the study of the inheritance of human characteristics through DNA, scientists have discovered more and more about both what we physically share with each other and about just how different we, as individuals, are from each other. Over the last ten years the DNA revolution and the study of human genetics has allowed us to know more and more about our past and about our relation to each other and to the rest of nature. The truth turns out to be that the idea of different 'races' is a nonsense. Skin colour, for example, has always been one of the most common ways in which people's race is said to be shown. But only about six genes control all the differences in skin colour to be seen in Europe and Africa, out of the 100,000 or so genes that make up each human being. Six out of a 100,000 is not much but people have hung on to this tiny cluster of differences the whole idea of 'race'. They have made them important even though the differences they show are literally 'only skin deep'.

But despite the fact that the idea of different races is no longer taken seriously by scientists, many people still suffer from being treated as a 'different race' and discriminated against. And it should be remembered that many people, including those who have been discriminated against, actually like to see themselves as members of a distinct race. So even though race isn't real, the fact that people treat race as real shows that it is, for the time being at least, a social fact, even if it isn't a biological one.

One aspect of human society that has been taken to show important differences between groups of people, and that is sometimes called 'racial', is the bundle of differences in language, religion, dress, eating habits and so on, that are in fact cultural or 'ethnic'. These sometimes correspond with people's geographical place in the world: people from South America, say, may not only share some inherited physical feature, such as straight black hair, but may also share certain languages in common, eat similar food or belong to the same religious groups.

Question

A person's culture is their ethnicity. So are we all 'ethnic' or not?

The idea of 'racial groups', even 'racial types' is sometimes used when people actually mean ethnic groups. And people frequently say 'racial' when they mean 'ethnic', or say 'ethnic' when they really mean 'of a certain skin colour'. In each case people's appearance and distinctive ways of being are used to classify and categorise. This is sometimes called 'stereotyping' - thinking that all people of a certain type have predictable characteristics and forms of behaviour.

This 'racial' and ethnic stereotyping also merges with national stereotyping: 'all French people eat garlic', 'all Germans are bossy', 'the Scots are a mean race', 'the Japanese are cruel', 'the English are cold and unfriendly'. Such national stereotypes can become 'racialised', that is, seen as really showing 'racial' differences between people, and this is often done by people wishing to justify themselves for treating certain groups of people in a particular way.

Europeans justified the taking of African people, transporting them and making them work as slaves in the Americas - North America, Central America, South America and the Caribbean - by saying that the 'African race' was not even fully human. Africans were 'inferior' and so it did not matter how they were treated.

A 19th-century engraving shows newly-captured African slaves held in chains and shackles to prevent their escape.

Question
Where do our ideas about groups of people who are different from us come from? Our parents? Our friends? TV? Politicians? Newspapers?

At other times British colonial rule was imposed on parts of India, and armies, police, and other instruments of 'law enforcement' were used and justified on the grounds that Indian 'races' were too unruly to govern themselves, that they needed the British to do the job for them. So the idea of 'race' has sometimes served the interests of people or governments who profited in different ways from the belief in 'races' and in their differences. The fact that great mineral wealth and other trading benefits, as well as international prestige were to be had from imposing European rule on the peoples of a distant country, did much to make the idea of racial difference and 'superiority' very popular with those nations who imposed themselves on others.

> **"I believe that the British race is the greatest of governing races the world has ever seen. I say this not merely as an empty boast, but as proved and shown by the success which we have had in administering vast dominions."**
>
> Joseph Chamberlain, *The Times*, 12 November, 1895

Science and Racism in the 19th Century

As the history of racism unfolded, the mistaken idea that there were several fundamentally different forms of human beings ('races') became increasingly useful to some people. When scientists in the 18th and 19th centuries thought they had discovered the principles of how human characteristics are carried down through families, and, therefore, so they thought, how 'races' are carried on from generation to generation, such a scientific backing was taken as proof that differences between rich countries and poor countries were the natural outcome of racial differences between the peoples of the world.

Other differences too, such as musical tastes or skill in sports, the arts and the sciences were taken to be because of race. Count Arthur Gobineau, a man later greatly admired by Adolf Hitler, wrote in the 19th century a book called 'Essay on the Inequality of Races' in which he argued that history was a struggle between the different 'races'. For him there were three races - the yellow, the black and the white, and he saw only the 'white race' as capable of having any civilisation. Several writers wrote books at that time introducing the then new idea that there were such things as races. Some said three, some said five different races, but even in those days, not everyone was convinced, and time has proved them right.

A craniometer, used in the 19th century to measure skulls. Such measurements were used by some scientists to support their theories about race.

'IT'S IN THE BLOOD' - OR IS IT?

Particularly in the 19th century scientists put a lot of effort into finding ways to establish what were the differences between the 'races of mankind'. The measurement of skulls was one of the ways scientists used to define racial types. Another common belief was that our 'racial inheritance' was carried in the blood. So ideas of being a 'pure-blooded Englishman', for example, or of someone having 'a bit of Spanish blood in her veins' became common metaphors for 'racial purity' and 'racial mixture'.

Ideas and expression such as these have become so much a part of our way of thinking and talking that it is often very hard to realise that the notion of genetic information being carried 'in the blood' - as opposed to within all of our cells - is just a way of picturing things. It was this idea of blood being the carrier of race that lay behind many kinds of racism, including the German Nazi Party's idea of a 'pure Aryan race', and the segregation of black and white people in Louisiana, USA through its 'Legislative Code III'. Under this law anyone with even 'one drop of negro blood' was to be classed as of the 'negro race'. They were not allowed to vote, go to certain schools or colleges, or enter certain places - however 'white' they looked. The so-called intermarriage of the races was seen as a 'mixing of the blood' that created confusion and a weakening of the 'stronger' races.

Question
'Racism is all about difference.' What do you think?

PREJUDICE AND DISCRIMINATION

'Prejudice' is a term often used in connection with racism. To be prejudiced means to pre-judge, to make up your mind about someone or something based on what you think you know before being better informed. And it's usually negative - you make your mind up against someone or some group. You may be prejudiced against people who come from the other side of town, or against pupils from another school, for example. Racial prejudice is deciding what you think about a person based on their skin colour, or what culture they come from.

There is, for example, a prejudice that Asians can't play soccer. Some talent scouts and team trainers believe that 'it's not part of Asian culture' or that 'Asians haven't got the build for football'. Yet there is a lot of football talent in the Asian community in Britain and the sport is so popular that there are several purely Asian football leagues in Britain. Many Asian youngsters would love a chance to show what they can do, but they mostly get passed over. It seems that prejudice is making people blind to these facts.

> " I remember in high school in New York I had a teacher who in front of the class used to call me 'swamp woman' because I was from the West Indies. That was supposed to be a big joke. But I didn't think it was so funny. People saying you live in shacks, you live in huts back there, or calling you 'coconut heads' and 'monkey chasers'. Which were some of the familiar terms in New York. "
>
> Margaret Prescod-Roberts, *Black Women: Bringing It All Back Home*, 1980

Despite the positive efforts of many football clubs to fight racism on the terraces, attendances at matches by ethnic minority groups is still very low.

'**Discrimination**' means treating one group of people differently from another. If someone is refused a job, or prevented from buying or renting a house because they are the 'wrong' colour, then that is racial discrimination. Discrimination is one of the ways racism works. It is one of the effects of racist ideas and attitudes.

So racism is two things: It is having certain ideas and attitudes *and* it is behaving in certain ways. A person can be racist in what they **think** (being prejudiced, for example) and in what they **do** (discriminating against people).

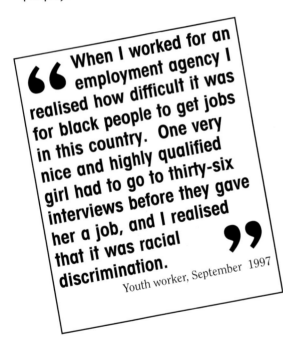

> When I worked for an employment agency I realised how difficult it was for black people to get jobs in this country. One very nice and highly qualified girl had to go to thirty-six interviews before they gave her a job, and I realised that it was racial discrimination.
>
> Youth worker, September 1997

Question

"It's only natural not to like people who look very different from us." Do you agree?

THE HOLOCAUST

Sometimes racism may be seen not only in how **people** act towards others but also how **governments** act. The most famous example of a racist government was when Germany was ruled by members of the Nazi Party in the 1930s and 1940s. The Nazis believed in the superiority of the white 'Aryan race' and set about a cruel programme of exterminating many thousands of people who were either not of that 'race' or who were believed to be weak or impure examples of it - those who were sick or suffered from physical disabilities, for example. Six million Jewish people, as well as gypsies and others, were put to death by the German state under Adolf Hitler. This tragedy came to be known as the Holocaust.

Anne Frank has become a symbol for many people through her diary. Her family fled from Germany after the rise of the Nazis, as did many other Jews after 1929. Anne's family moved to Holland but the spread of Fascist ideas in Europe caught them in a trap as Jewish people were being 'cleaned away'. Anne Frank kept a diary while she and her family hid in a sealed-up annexe to a building owned by her father. Her diary records her daily life and growing up until the time the family were discovered and deported to a concentration camp. She died aged sixteen in the camp but her diary was published after her death. It has had a great impact on children and adults all over the world.

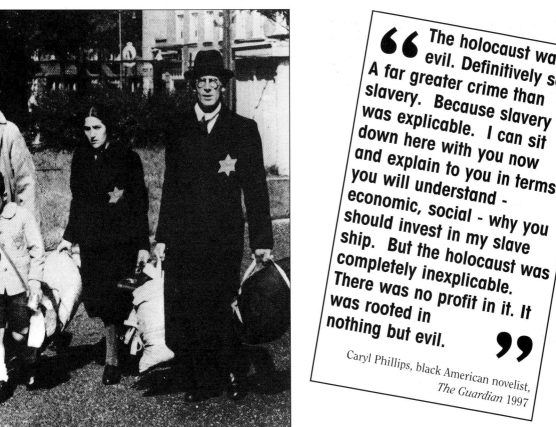

Many Jews were forced to wear the yellow Star of David to identify them and families were continually uprooted.

> "The holocaust was evil. Definitively so. A far greater crime than slavery. Because slavery was explicable. I can sit down here with you now and explain to you in terms you will understand - economic, social - why you should invest in my slave ship. But the holocaust was completely inexplicable. There was no profit in it. It was rooted in nothing but evil."
>
> Caryl Phillips, black American novelist, *The Guardian* 1997

> "Saturday 20 June 1942. Anti-Jewish decrees followed each other in quick succession. Jews must wear a yellow star, Jews must hand in their bicycles, Jews are banned from trains and are forbidden to drive. Jews are only allowed to do their shopping between three and five o'clock and then only in shops which bear the placard 'Jewish shop'. Jews must be indoors by eight o'clock and cannot even sit in their own gardens after that hour..."
>
> Anne Frank, *The Diary of a Young Girl*, 1953

DISCRIMINATION IN AFRICA AND AMERICA...

The system of apartheid ('apartness') in South Africa, which segregated whites and non-whites, was finally demolished in the early 1990s.

For many years the white South African government followed a deliberately racist policy maintaining strict laws that kept the black majority powerless and discriminated against in education, housing, employment, health, welfare and in many other respects. Legal and voting rights were also very restricted. This was known as the apartheid system. Under this system, black people were segregated from white people on public transport, and in public places such as beaches and parks. They were not allowed to marry white people, and very little land was available for purchase by black people, even if they could have afforded it. Black children were educated separately. Black adults had to carry a passbook to allow them to move about in 'white' areas.

In the southern states of the USA, following the American Civil War and right through to the 1960s, there were laws that restricted the rights of black people from doing many of the things permitted to white people. These state laws forbade black and white children from attending the same schools and colleges, and the same laws kept black people from voting, from sharing public transport facilities, from eating in the same restaurants. These were known as 'segregation' - nick-named 'Jim Crow' - laws. They were a form of legal, official discrimination.

...AND IN JAPAN

Koreans are the largest ethnic minority in Japan but there have long been popular prejudices against them. They were once - when Japan occupied Korea in the early 20th century - regarded as 'Imperial Subjects' and were conscripted for forced labour in coal mines, armament factories and in military service. After the Second World War they were deprived of Japanese citizenship, but circumstances forced most of them to remain in Japan.

> Second and third generations of Koreans were born and grew up in Japan, speaking the Japanese language, going to Japanese schools, working and getting married in Japan and paying taxes. But unless they naturalised as Japanese they were not entitled to even the most basic rights. Many Koreans in Japan have faced discrimination concerning marriage, employment, housing and other social aspects.
>
> Yasumasa Hirasawa,
> *World Yearbook of Education 1997*

RELIGION AND RACISM

> A report from the Commission for Racial Equality published in 1997 states that southern Irish people suffer high levels of prejudice and discrimination in the UK.

Sometimes prejudice against certain religions becomes combined with racism. Both forms of prejudice can also exist independently of each other. The conflict between Protestants and Catholics in Ireland, for example, cannot really be considered as racial conflict. But what of the suspicions and stereotypical images that non-Muslims have of Muslims?

Muslims in many countries feel that they are discriminated against in employment, education and in society in general because they have a different religion. In European countries, Muslims who are not white feel that they are discriminated against on religious as well as racial grounds. Hence Turks in Germany, North Africans in France and Pakistanis and Bangladeshis in Britain all complain of double discrimination. In 1996, Vijay Singh, a Sikh boy living in Manchester, was driven to hang himself because of bullying. He had been taunted on the football pitch because of his Sikh turban, and never saw Manchester United play because of his parents' fear of racism on the terraces. It is often difficult to sort out religious prejudice from racial as they often overlap and one can become an excuse for the other.

Muslim girls and women who have to wear traditional clothes and cover their bodies are particularly vulnerable to racial and religious prejudices.

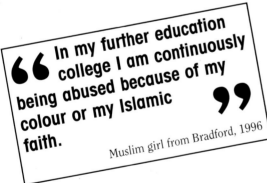

66 In my further education college I am continuously being abused because of my colour or my Islamic faith. 99

Muslim girl from Bradford, 1996

Find out!
Find out what action is being taken to fight racism in sport locally and nationally.

WHAT IS THE LINK BETWEEN EXPLORATION AND RACISM?

2540
305.8

One thing that influences how we view people is how we see the world. Often we see those who live in the countries that are near to our own as being most like us. Those who come from distant places with different climates we may see as not like us at all. Sometimes, of course, people from one country really don't like people from the country only next door! On the other hand such things may not influence us. We may see the world as full of people who are all more or less just like us.

Question
Have you ever been to another country? Did you feel 'out of place' or were you surprised at how familiar things were? What kinds of things made a difference to you feeling at home or not?

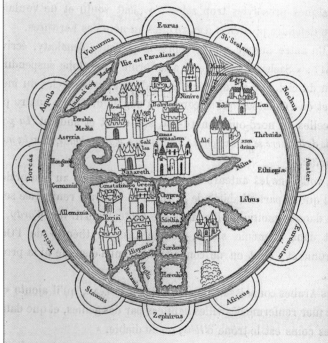

A 14th-century map of the world showing Jerusalem at the centre.

OF MAPS AND MYTHS

Before information about the world and its geography was fully documented, the maps made by people often reflected both their knowledge of and their fears about distant places. Far corners of the earth were said to be full of strange and dangerous creatures, wild tribes and ferocious monsters.

Gradually, as more and more voyages of discovery were made, and better measuring techniques developed, new and better-informed maps began to be made. But the world could still be drawn from any point of view. With a globe you can start your map and divide it up in almost anyway that is convenient for what you want to show. One Arab map from the 13th century shows the world with north at the bottom and south at the top. It looks very strange to our eyes but it's not inaccurate. It is just another way of showing things. Religious map-makers would put their holy city - Jerusalem or Mecca, for example - at the centre of the world. One 6th-century Babylonian map of the known world engraved on a clay tablet shows Babylon at the centre and the outer regions inhabited by legendary beings. If you think that where you live is the most important place on earth you are likely to put it right in the middle and this is exactly what the European map-makers also tended to do as first the Portuguese then the Spanish, Dutch, British and French explorers informed other Europeans about the parts of world they 'discovered'.

EUROCENTRISM

European map-making really took off in the period when most European voyages of discovery were made - the 15th to 18th centuries. And just as trade with distant peoples followed discovery, so conquest also often followed trade.

During these crucial centuries 'Eurocentrism' - seeing all the world and its peoples from a European point of view - became established and the year 1492 - when Columbus landed in the Americas - marks a key moment in that process. From that point on knowledge of the world became less and less a humble knowledge of the rich variety to be found in

An early 17th-century painting of a slave market in a European settlement in America.

the universe, and more and more a proclamation of the uniqueness and superiority of the European nations, their religion, their science, their languages, their arts. The imagined map of the world for Europeans - the ways Europeans came to think about and picture the world - saw the peoples who inhabited these newly 'discovered' places as having one important thing in common - they were all regarded as 'other', 'savage' not 'civilised', often regarded as 'dirty' not 'clean', 'wild' not 'tame', being part of 'nature' (like the animals), not part of 'culture' (like the Europeans). These ways of thinking have continued down the years, as the following quotation shows:

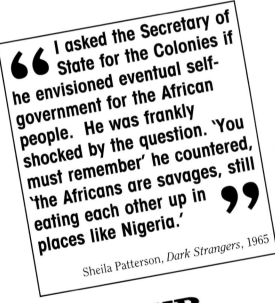

I asked the Secretary of State for the Colonies if he envisioned eventual self-government for the African people. He was frankly shocked by the question. 'You must remember' he countered, 'the Africans are savages, still eating each other up in places like Nigeria.'

Sheila Patterson, *Dark Strangers*, 1965

1492 AND ALL THAT

The special moment in history that is marked by the date 1492 is worth looking at. Columbus found lands unknown to Europeans but these were not, of course, a 'New World' but another 'Old World', with its own long and important history. Neither Columbus nor Europeans generally recognised this. The peoples of the Americas were regarded as natural objects - another 'resource' to be discovered and exploited - not human beings with histories as worthy as those of Europe.

Question

Can you think of any examples in the modern world where people of one ethnic or 'racial' group are economically exploited, or is all that a thing of the past?

Europeans also failed to realise how fragile the American environment was. The resources of the 'New World' were despoiled and its peoples of diverse cultures often destroyed. This is how it happened: After Columbus' first voyage, a ship called 'Admiral of the Ocean' returned in September 1493 with seventeen other ships to Hispanola - the Caribbean island we know today as Haiti and the Dominican Republic - and unloaded 1500 people, together with plants and animals - horses, cows, pigs, wheat, barley, shoots of sugar cane etc. - most of which affected the environment in very bad ways. Sugar cane, for example, was bad for both the land - the tropical rain forest which was cut down to make space for the sugar plantations - and for people. The growing and cutting of sugar cane needs large numbers of people to do the work at very low or even no cost. So it was bad for both the local people who were soon wiped out by the hardships of forced labour in the fields, and by the various illnesses that the Europeans accidentally brought with them in their own bodies and in their plants and animals. The indigenous population had

never been exposed to these illnesses before and had no immunity to them. It was also in the end disastrous for the millions of Africans who were captured and brought to the 'New World' as slaves to work in the plantations.

Find out!

What has happened to the people who live in the tropical rainforests today? How are they and their environment treated? Do you think this has anything to do with racism?

SOLD INTO SLAVERY

Plantations - not just of sugar cane but of maize, cotton and potatoes as well - completely changed the Americas. The growing of crops on this great scale required many, many workers. Indeed the plantation system was always hungry for workers. Starting with local peoples, the system was quickly forced to turn to workers from anywhere. And nearly always it was workers who cost little or nothing. This, of course, meant slavery. Slaves were bought and sold like objects. They cost a certain amount of money to buy, and after that were maintained as cheaply as possible. Millions of plantation workers were kept in slavery on the assumption that they were not human beings at all. It is estimated that between ten and thirty million people, mostly from Africa, were sold in the Americas. At the same time, the ancient civilizations of central America and their peoples were turned into marginalised groups without rights or dignity in their own lands.

In this way at least two geographically different groups of peoples - the local native peoples and those brought as slaves from Africa - became affected by the Europeans' desire to get rich and have command over distant parts of the world.

So looking at the world through 'European lenses' became not just a matter of how things were viewed, but it actually affected people - those who lived and worked in those places that became the objects of Discovery-Trade-Conquest - in their daily lives.

Today people all over the world still suffer from the pictures of them conjured up through the maps, travellers' exaggerated tales and artists' imaginings of the past. Those images of strange and 'savage' peoples from distant countries and 'other races' are part of what makes racism so difficult to get away from. They have become part of how people's 'differences' may still be seen - even when we know better.

Question

Do you think that racism in the past has had a lasting effect on some groups of people? If so, how?

Question

If a big company or a government is legally proved to have injured someone in the past - such as by permitting dangerous work practices - that company or that government has to compensate the person or their family. Should countries that have used slavery in the past compensate their black populations for the effects of slavery?

WHAT ARE THE EFFECTS OF RACISM ON EDUCATION?

Racism may have its roots way back in history but its effects today are what concern us most. Its effects on young people are particularly worrying - especially when it affects learning. It can affect learning in very many ways, some big and dramatic and others apparently small. All can have a lasting effect on young people.

RACIAL HARASSMENT

In Britain, racial harassment and even assault are frequently experienced by children and young people. Sometimes this takes the form of racist name-calling, sometimes it is more physical.

There have even been racist murders perpetrated against ethnic minority pupils. The report of the Macdonald Inquiry into racism and racial violence in schools in Manchester was called 'Murder in the Playground'. It followed the murder of 13-year-old Ahmed Iqbal Ullah who was knifed in his school playground by a white pupil.

How do some schools manage better than others in removing racism from the classroom?

> ❝ **When I came to this country I thought everything would be good and fine but when I went to school everyone was being racist to me. Some of them would say 'Hey, Hamed, why are you black? I know why you're black. It's because you never had a wash since you were born'. And they say to me 'You black bastard, what are you doing in this country? You should go back to where you came from.'** ❞
>
> A teenage refugee drom Somalia, *Routes of Racism*, video

> ❝ **I gave birth to my daughter - and my daughter's of mixed race - to prove the fact that we can love each other in this world and we can all get on together. But it's hard... My daughter had her nose broken, then they started throwing broken bottles at her. Now she gets racism from children from eight to fourteen... and we live in fear.** ❞
>
> A (white) mother, *Routes of Racism*, video

More recently there have been other racial murders of young students in the UK. Although these have mainly been perpetrated against black and Asian young people, racially motivated attacks on whites are not unknown, though rare. It is mainly the black and ethnic minority communities that have come to live in fear of violent attack, so that much smaller instances of harassment, like name calling, come to cause a high level of anxiety. Sometimes racist graffiti is deliberately used to create this atmosphere of uncertainty and terror.

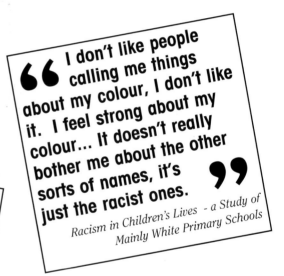

> ❝ **I don't like people calling me things about my colour, I don't like it. I feel strong about my colour... It doesn't really bother me about the other sorts of names, it's just the racist ones.** ❞
>
> *Racism in Children's Lives - a Study of Mainly White Primary Schools*

Racism by children and young people against other children and young people is one of the most common forms of everyday racism in many cities across Europe. It turns childhood into a nightmare of bullying and fear, it makes young people afraid to leave their homes and so restricts their leisure activities as well as undermining their school work. So it can badly affect their futures.

Children of mixed parentage sometimes feel that they are treated by their peers as not belonging to any group.

> ❝ My mum is from the Philippines and my dad's English. But people are not interested in that and show their ignorance by calling me 'chinky' at school, and going on about slanting eyes. I wish that everyone was like my mum and dad. They love each other even though they come from totally different backgrounds and cultures. ❞
>
> Tom, 14, Edinburgh

Question
The challenge is to re-educate the minority of young people who are guilty of racist harassment. How do you think this could be done?

In the United States it has even happened that some white pupils with black friends have been subjected to abuse, especially those who have adopted 'black' Hip Hop styles of dress. At a high school in Indiana a group of white girls were harassed by fellow students for 'acting black'. The students also said that Ku Klux Klan and 'White Power' slogans had been daubed on their lockers and several of them said they were spat on by male students.

The Ku Klux Klan, formed by white Americans in the 19th century to fight against black and other ethnic minority groups, still campaign today, but are far fewer in number.

Find out!
Have your local schools got special rules to deal with racist bullying? If so, what are they? Can you think how they might be improved?

Question
What kinds of things can lead to racial violence and bullying in schools?

SEGREGATION IN SCHOOL

Question
'Racism in schools and colleges is not just about bullying, it's also about the quality of education received, what subjects are taught, how respectfully the home languages and religions of school students are treated.' What do you think?

In certain parts of the United States up until the successes of the Civil Rights Movement, schools were legally segregated. That is to say, there were schools for white children and other schools for black children. Schools could not provide an education for both 'races' learning together. Furthermore, it was the schools for white children that had the best buildings, books and equipment, the best qualified teachers and could provide the best education. This meant that white students got better examination results, went on to better jobs and, as adults, could then live in better neighbourhoods and, in turn, send their children to better schools. In this way racism in education affected far more than just what went on in schools. It affected the whole of American society.

A school for black children in a southern state of the USA, in the 1940s

Question
'If a kid is bright s/he'll learn whatever the school is like.' What do you think?

Following an important legal case known as Brown v the Board of Education, in 1954, schools gradually became permitted to admit whoever they chose regardless of race. However, very many schools are still often divided into black schools and white schools, not because of the law but because of social factors. Black school students are often isolated in poor areas because the long history of racial oppression has affected the overall economic position of black Americans as a group. In some ways schools in the United States are even more segregated than they were forty years ago.

If a school has an ethnically diverse intake of students, then the way the school curriculum deals with the variety of cultures, and how teachers behave towards the students, can affect seriously how comfortable students feel, how well they learn, and how complete an education they receive. A school that only shows respect for one culture may be said to be ethnically or 'racially' biased. In other words, racism can also show itself in small but important matters.

Question
Should the national curriculum reflect the variety of cultures represented by the student population of this country?

Question
Should all religions be treated with equal respect in schools in multicultural societies? Should all religious groups in a school be allowed to celebrate their own religious festivals?

NATIONS AND NATIONALISM

Racism is sometimes associated with nationalism - a strong belief in the importance of one's own country. Attachment to our own country - whether that means the country where we were born, or the country we have come to live in - can be a perfectly good thing. On the other hand, it has often been the cause of wars as countries compete for dominance and influence in the world. Unfortunately it is also often bound up with beliefs about who should be counted as a member of a country and who should not - who's in and who should be kept out.

Many modern states have developed out of groups of much smaller countries where people tended to speak the same or similar languages. Italy or Germany in the mid-19th century, for example, did not exist as single countries but were formed from a number of small self-governing states. Where one country ends and another begins seems fairly simple when the country is also an island, but quite often it is just a matter of chance as to where a line gets drawn between two 'countries'. Those who are 'in' and those who are 'out' might be very similar, even identical to each other. Most countries are actually made up of many different ethnic groups as well as being rather blurry at the edges.

Question
What does your country's flag mean to you?

Flags flying outside the United Nations building in New York. What does a nation's flag mean to its people?

BLOOD AND SOIL

People come to feel that they are attached to a certain country by birth - it's where they and other members of their family were born - and they feel themselves to be part of the history and culture of that country. Sometimes this way of identifying with a country leads people into thinking that some members have more of a right to belong than others.

In countries where several ethnic groups live in little pockets near each other - such as in the area formerly known as Yugoslavia - conflicts can arise that lead to wars and to the expelling of those who suddenly find themselves regarded as 'outsiders' when a new government draws the line around the country in a new way. Removing those who are no longer considered as belonging has sometimes been called 'ethnic cleansing'. In the name of

The former Yugoslavia was the home of six separate national groups. As each fought bitterly for independence, more than four million refugees were forced to leave their homes.

'ethnic cleansing', people have been driven from their homes, imprisoned, tortured and executed. It is exactly this kind of discrimination, prejudice and cruelty that marks it out as a form of racism. Like the experience of the Jews in Nazi Germany, it shows how racism and nationalism can join together.

Question
'It's only natural for people to love their country and not like outsiders.' What do you think?

Question
Are all wars basically 'ethnic' or 'racial' conflicts?

'LIBERTY, EQUALITY, FRATERNITY'

The idea of a unified country does not have to be so bound up with exaggerating differences between people and deciding who belongs and who is 'foreign'. French nationalism after the French Revolution of 1789 was founded on the ideas of 'liberty, equality, and fraternity'. These ideas were also taken up into the formation of the constitution of the United States - a country where many different ethnic groups live, eager to regard themselves and other groups as American citizens. In these countries, at least in theory, a person can be a citizen whatever their origin. So a 'nationality' can be a kind of umbrella under which differences can come together. Even if it doesn't always work out that way, it can be

a useful way to think about living in the modern world without conflict - and something good to aim for. So nationalism doesn't have to be about excluding people who 'don't belong', it can also be about inclusion and diversity - celebrating belonging to a country that includes many different traditions, religions and languages or even mixes them up into a new modern blend.

A BILL OF RIGHTS

A Bill of Rights is a legally binding, government-authorised list of human rights. Citizens in most countries have fundamental rights and freedoms. In Britain at the present time the Race Relations Act 1976 and Sex Discrimination Act 1975 provide protection to minorities and women through law. However, some people have argued strongly for an extension to these acts in a Human Rights Act and such an Act will come into force in the UK in 2000. For many years anyone in Britain who wanted redress to the violation of their rights has had to take the case to the European Court of Human Rights.

Question
Do you think that being bound together in a common struggle can cause people to share similar values?

Despite having a Bill of Rights, both America and France have been countries well known for racism and racial problems. So it isn't like a magic wand to wave at racism and make it go away, although it can help in the fight against racism if there is an inclusive idea of 'the nation', rather than an exclusive one.

Chapter 5

IMMIGRATION, RACE AND NATION

Governments often set up rules about who can enter their countries to settle down and live. These rules are supposed to ensure that the population of a particular country manages to support itself economically - that there are enough resources of, say, jobs, health care and education to go round for everyone.

However, these rules are not always operated fairly. In particular, these rules maybe racist, either in how they are written or in how they are applied. A government may say that it is only concerned about economics when it excludes those who wish to enter the country, but when people of some ethnic or 'racial' groups are excluded while others are allowed in, then this may be at best only a half-truth. The other 'half' is that racism may be at work.

A police officer in New York attempts to arrest a demonstrator protesting against the acquittal of four officers accused of beating up a black motorist.

Australia did not bother with even this 'half-truth'. It had a racist 'White Australia' policy from 1901 to 1966 which excluded black people and Asians, as well as other groups of Mediterranean origin. Of course native Australians - the Aborigines - were hardly recognised as part of the 'nation'. In time, however, Australia came to abandon these crude policies. Nowadays it is far more multicultural.

Canada also has a native population who are a minority in their own land and whose legal rights were for a long time fewer than those of the white French and English-speaking people who colonised their country. Here, too, there has been a history of 'whites only' immigration. In May 1914 the ship *Komagata Maru* with 376 East Indian passengers was denied entry by the authorities at Vancouver and its passengers suffered brutal assaults. Gradually, Canada also became far more racially mixed. In the 1950s and 60s larger numbers of people were needed to work in both skilled and unskilled jobs. Thousands of Europeans from Holland, Germany, Italy, Greece and Portugal moved there. By 1988 the numbers entering were about 135,000 and included immigrants from non-European backgrounds.

In Canada the society is considered to be multicultural. A Multicultural Directorate was set up in 1976. Most provinces also have policies on multiculturalism and human rights commissions. Issues of racism are also dealt with by provincial and federal governments and language teaching undertaken through heritage language programmes.

In Great Britain in 1968 the Conservative Member of Parliament Enoch Powell delivered a speech against black and Asian

Native Australians still struggle for rights in their own land.

immigration in which he tried to create a fear amongst white British people that if immigration by these groups did not cease Britain would become like a vast river 'foaming with much blood'. The speech stirred up a lot of racism and hatred. In the same year the Labour government passed a new law, the Commonwealth Immigration Act, which denied permanent entry to anyone who did not have at least one grandparent who was born in Britain. This effectively excluded most people from the new Commonwealth. The law of course did not say 'no black people allowed', but that was its effect. The mood of the time was one of anxiety amongst the white population about 'immigration' - though not about immigration from predominantly 'white' countries like Australia, New Zealand and Canada. Enoch Powell's speech was not concerned with limiting entry for people from those countries.

Many white British voters were expressing fears about 'coloured immigrants' and it was those fears that the Act was responding to. The actual figures for the 'coloured population' resident in England and Wales given in a 1966 census - which included people from the Caribbean, the Indian sub-

Today's young children are more likely than previous generations in the UK to expect a wide variety of ethnic origin in their schools.

continent, British West Africa and the Far East - were a total of 710,900. The same census also included people whose parents came from those regions but who were themselves born in the United Kingdom. (These people were not, of course, immigrants, but the children of immigrants.)

This group totalled 213,300. So the grand total of 'coloured' people was 924,000 for the whole of England and Wales. The way the word 'immigrants' was used was itself a sign of the times. People often said 'immigrants' when they meant 'black people'. They didn't mean Australians or Germans or Swedes. Black voters at that time were far fewer in number and their fears - which were more about racial assaults and accommodation and employment difficulties - did not have a visible impact on the politicians of the day. It was not until eight years later, in 1976, that the Race Relations Act was passed addressing some of the problems of racism faced by black people.

RACE RELATIONS

The Race Relations Act of 1976 granted powers to set up the Commission for Racial Equality. The Home Secretary appoints the Commissioners and has support from all the main political parties. The purpose of the Commission is to improve relations between all racial groups and to eliminate racism. The Race Relations Act makes racial discrimination unlawful in employment, training, housing, education and provision of goods, facilities and services. Racial discrimination may be direct if people are treated unfairly on grounds of race,

nationality, citizenship, ethnic or national origin. Racial discrimination can also be indirect, when a rule or policy puts people from particular backgrounds at a disadvantage. If, for instance, a company makes British university qualifications compulsory for managerial vacancies, this would exclude all candidates from overseas with overseas qualifications.

Question
Discrimination on grounds of religion is not included under the current Race Relations Act. Do you think it should be?

In Australia, Canada and Great Britain, times have changed and so have the laws. Some people think for the better and some, for the worse. But laws about who's in and who's out are quickly written, and if the politicians of any country feel there is a new need to exclude a group - either because they genuinely feel there is a threat to the economy or to social order, or because large numbers of voters have given voice to fears about some new immigrant group - then even tomorrow new immigration laws can come into existence. So racist immigration laws are not just a part of distant history. They are still part of modern life.

Question
Are there fair and unfair ways of making immigration laws?

Find out!
Have there been any new immigration laws in this country in the last five years? What are they?

Question

If a country has one official religion what freedoms should people of other religions have?

Question

Should different ethnic groups be forced to mix with each other or should they be allowed to live totally separately if they choose to?

Find out!

Find out about the Commission for Racial Equality and the work it does.

Find out!

Find out about recent cases taken to court under the Race Relations Act.

RACISM ON THE MOVE
NOMADS, MIGRANTS AND SETTLERS

People who change their country, cross borders to live somewhere else, or simply have a nomadic way of life, often suffer from racism. This seems to be for at least two reasons: (1) people are easily made to fear and distrust 'outsiders'; and (2) those who move frequently and therefore don't carry many possessions with them (such as nomads) sometimes become thought of as 'lawless'. This is what some people thought about the North American 'Indian' tribes (native Americans), the Bushmen of southern Africa and the native peoples of Australia, amongst many others.

For as long as humans have lived on this earth, however, people have lived as nomads. In fact for about 85 per cent of the time since the last ice age, humans have lived in this way. It is only relatively recently in the long history of the world that humans have settled in permanent villages, towns and cities.

There are many reasons why different groups of people are 'on the move' nowadays. Some move from one country to another to find work. Many people are forced on the move because of wars. There are many such

Boat people - people who leave their native land unofficially by boat - are particularly vulnerable - even to modern-day pirates.

refugees - which means people taking 'refuge' (shelter) in countries not their own - in the world today. Others, like the Gypsies, move because they still try to live in their traditional way, moving about as the flow of seasonal work changes.

Question
How many reasons can you think of why a family should wish or have to move from country to country?

Question
"When in Rome do as the Romans do." If people move to another country do you think they have a responsibility to change their ways to be more like the people whose country they have moved to?

Find out!
How much did the British colonists who went to Africa, India, Australia or America, change their ways to fit in with the native peoples?

Most of these reasons for moving from place to place and country to country have also been true for hundreds and thousands of years: the ancient tribes of Europe, the sea-faring people of the Pacific islands, the Eskimos following the reindeer, the Arab trading peoples, refugees from war-torn cities described in the Bible and in the old Greek epics and plays. Yet, many people on the move still suffer from hostility and even physical attack from people in the neighbourhoods where they pass through, take refuge, or try to build a new life for themselves.

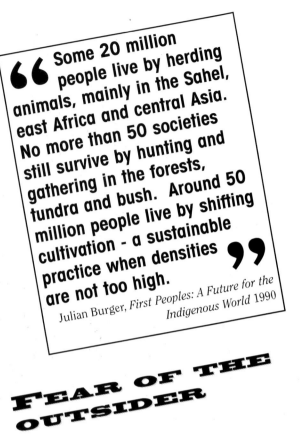

66 Some 20 million people live by herding animals, mainly in the Sahel, east Africa and central Asia. No more than 50 societies still survive by hunting and gathering in the forests, tundra and bush. Around 50 million people live by shifting cultivation - a sustainable practice when densities are not too high. 99

Julian Burger, *First Peoples: A Future for the Indigenous World* 1990

FEAR OF THE OUTSIDER

The Gypsies are a clear example of 'fear of the outsider', because for settled peoples they always are 'outsiders' and so they have suffered persecution for hundreds of years. They left north India - probably in the 10th century - and by the beginning of the 14th century they had moved through Persia and Anatolia to places such as Crete, Corfu, Serbia, Romania, Croatia and Bohemia. In Western Europe they were sometimes referred to as 'Bohemians' but people came to call them 'Gypsies' as a shortening of 'Egyptian' because they were thought to have come from Egypt.

When they arrived in a new place they were sometimes greeted with a welcome as well as astonishment at their life-style, unusual

Gypsies at a festival in southern France. Gypsies have been persecuted for centuries.

appearance and the entertainments - bear-dancing, juggling and so on - they put on. However, hostility towards them also seems to have grown once the novelty wore off and they came to be regarded as thieves and cut-throats. There were gypsy hunts with bounty if they were captured, they were banished from one country after another, and in Romania they were reduced to slavery in the 14th century which continued until 1856. They were persecuted and imprisoned in Tudor England during the 16th century, and finally there are estimates that from 250,000 to 400,000 of them were put to death by the Nazis in the concentration camps between 1943 and 1945.

Gypsies seem not to 'belong' anywhere but they are a people of great self-sufficiency.

" I hate these Gypsies. Why can't they stay in their own country instead of coming over here and taking up the houses that should be there for us? "

Kentish woman after the arrival of numbers of Gypsies from the Czech Republic fleeing from persecution in their own country, October 1997

They are very unusual in never being bounded by a territory. They have a flexible identity not attached to any particular piece of earth. Some say that 'the land they belong to lies inside themselves' and to that they always belong. Perhaps this has given them the strength to endure the racism they have suffered through the centuries. For those of us who are not Gypsies, their lives may help us to think about what 'belongingness' might mean for us and for others.

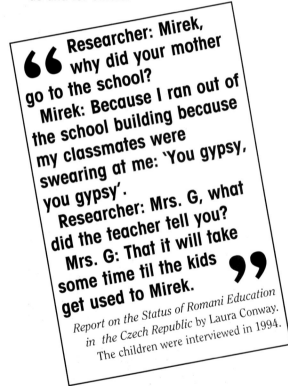

"Researcher: Mirek, why did your mother go to the school?
Mirek: Because I ran out of the school building because my classmates were swearing at me: 'You gypsy, you gypsy'.
Researcher: Mrs. G, what did the teacher tell you?
Mrs. G: That it will take some time til the kids get used to Mirek."

Report on the Status of Romani Education in the Czech Republic by Laura Conway. The children were interviewed in 1994.

Find out!
Ask members of your family from different generations what they think it means to 'belong to a place'.

OUTSIDE THE LAW IN AFRICA

Another group of nomadic people once regarded as living 'outside the law' is the San, long known as the 'Bushmen' of southern Africa. These hunters and gatherers once occupied the whole of southern Africa. Now there are just a handful of Bushman bands. For thousands of years they had the place entirely to themselves and within their own small areas small bands of people would move about following the supply of animals and food for gathering. Gradually other - tribal - people moved from the north into their region, but they seem to have lived side by side with some success.

Once the Europeans landed near Cape Town in the 17th century however, their fate was sealed. Over the next two hundred years they were themselves hunted like animals by the white settlers, who came from Holland and Britain. Raiding parties would go out at dawn, surround a group of huts and open fire, killing all the men, women and children while they slept. The records of these 'commando raids' against this very peaceable people make very sad reading. By the end of the 19th century they had been almost completely wiped out, or driven into some of the most inhospitable places to live.

The San lived very close to nature. They had great and detailed knowledge of animals and plants and a wonderful musical and oral culture of dances, songs and stories. They were also great artists, as many hundreds of rock shelters covered with beautiful San

paintings of animals and hunting scenes show. Despite their fine culture, however, they were mostly regarded by the Europeans as 'wild', 'like the animals', without property and without law. They were called 'Bushmen' by the whites because they lived 'in the bushes' and didn't have 'real' homes. In fact these European settlers - though they were very far from their own country of origin - did not regard the San as 'civilized' at all. So much did they see them as the 'lowest race of human beings' that they seemed to have no conscience about killing them without mercy.

This was a very vicious form of racism but many nomadic peoples and others living close to nature have suffered similarly. For example, the native American 'Indians' of North, South and Central America have also suffered massacre and near extermination.

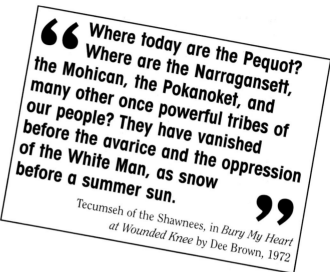

" Where today are the Pequot? Where are the Narragansett, the Mohican, the Pokanoket, and many other once powerful tribes of our people? They have vanished before the avarice and the oppression of the White Man, as snow before a summer sun. "

Tecumseh of the Shawnees, in *Bury My Heart at Wounded Knee* by Dee Brown, 1972

By the early 20th century the San, who had occupied southern Africa for many thousands of years - in fact no one has ever discovered an earlier people there - were all but exterminated. Small bands continue to this day in Botswana but they number very few.

Find out!
What countries have nomads nowadays and how are the nomads treated by their governments?

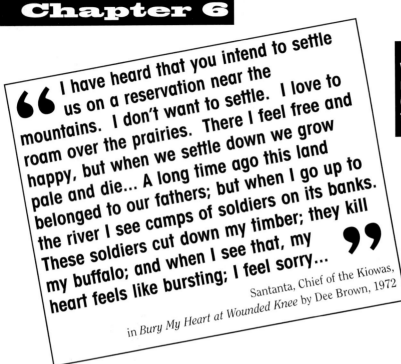

" I have heard that you intend to settle us on a reservation near the mountains. I don't want to settle. I love to roam over the prairies. There I feel free and happy, but when we settle down we grow pale and die... A long time ago this land belonged to our fathers; but when I go up to the river I see camps of soldiers on its banks. These soldiers cut down my timber; they kill my buffalo; and when I see that, my heart feels like bursting; I feel sorry... "

Santanta, Chief of the Kiowas,

in *Bury My Heart at Wounded Knee* by Dee Brown, 1972

It is now recognised that native Americans were cheated out of many of their lands because they believed that the land 'belonged' to no one.

RACISM IN THE WORKPLACE

Some people think that at least one kind of racism actually started 'in the workplace' - if you consider a slave-plantation a 'workplace'. The reason is simple: slaves were not captured for their colour but for their strength. But some argue that once the Africans, who were considered fast and strong, had been enslaved by European and Arab slave traders, racism almost grew out of the economics of slavery.

Some experts think that money, how people make a living, lies at the bottom of most forms of racism.

> **Nearly four in ten young black women were unemployed in 1995/6 compared with just over one in ten young white women.**

Like schools, workplaces are increasingly multi-ethnic. Making sure that racism does not play a part in working life is a problem for many workers and managers.

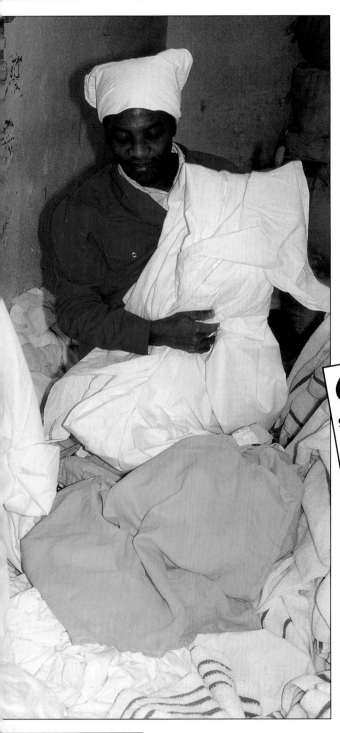

These are some of the questions to consider about racism in the workplace:

• Do all races have a fair chance in getting all jobs?

• Do the 'top jobs' only go to one main racial group?

• If people are discriminated against in job interviews, how does this happen?

• Are people of certain ethnic groups treated the same as everyone else in their jobs? Do they all get the same pay for the same job? Do they all have the same rights?

> " Letters from a black and a white applicant were sent to a well-known bank in Glasgow enquiring about vacancies. The white applicant received an application form, while the black applicant was told that there were no suitable openings. "

(left and opposite) What factors do you think influence the differing degrees of success at work between people of the same, and different, backgrounds?

> A retailer in the Merseyside area informed the black and the Asian applicants that the sales vacancy they had applied to had been filled. On the same day, the white, Irish and Chinese applicants received letters inviting them for interviews.

RACE AND UNEMPLOYMENT

If we look at the unemployment statistics for any country we also get another picture of racism in the workplace. For example, if more people in a certain minority group are unemployed compared with the number of unemployed in the majority group, you might wonder if the cause is to do with racism in any way.

It may and it may not, or at least not directly. It could be that at interviews people in the minority group were discriminated against by prejudiced interviewers, or it could be that high academic qualifications were required and many of those in the minority group didn't have the right ones.

Figures for unemployment and ethnicity in the UK, 1996/7:

	Unemployed
African	28%
Bangladeshi	27%
Caribbean	28%
Indian	13%
Pakistani	27%
White	9%

Source: Labour Force Survey

On the other hand, perhaps racism had worked in the education system so that people from the minorities didn't get a good enough education to get the qualifications needed for the jobs. In South Africa, for many years black children were provided with a much poorer education than that of the ruling white group. Their teachers were not so well qualified, the schools had fewer and older books, scientific equipment was rarely available. In consequence, under this racist apartheid system, the lowest paid work

Inside a gold mine in South Africa, before the end of apartheid. Who gives the orders and who takes them can be a clear guide to racism in the workplace.

went to the young black men straight out of school whose education had not fitted them for anything better.

The same was true in the United States of America, although in a slightly more subtle form. In the southern states of the USA workers were often hired on the basis of colour. The blacker you were, the less likely to get a job. As it says in the words of this old blues song, recorded by the famous black blues singer, Big Bill Broonzy:

> If you're white you're all right
> If you're brown stick around
> But if you're black, oh brother
> get back, get back, get back.

Today there are lots of ways that racism can be seen in relation to unemployment, work and work conditions.

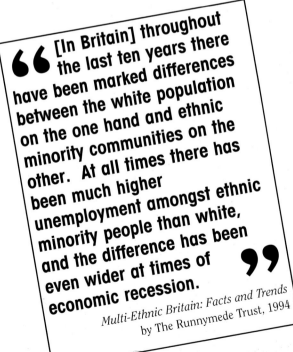

66 [In Britain] throughout the last ten years there have been marked differences between the white population on the one hand and ethnic minority communities on the other. At all times there has been much higher unemployment amongst ethnic minority people than white, and the difference has been even wider at times of economic recession. 99

Multi-Ethnic Britain: Facts and Trends
by The Runnymede Trust, 1994

Question
In some countries there have been laws that force employers to operate a quota system. This means if there is 12 per cent of a certain minority in a city then that should be reflected in the numbers of people of that ethnicity employed in the workplace. Do you think that is a good way to make sure that employment is not ethnically or racially biased?

MISERY AT WORK...

There are many cases of racial discrimination in the workplace every year. Some are taken to special tribunals designed to protect people against racial discrimination. The main law that is used in Britain is known as the Race Relations Act of 1976, which makes it a legal offence to discriminate against people on grounds of race or ethnicity.

Sometimes it takes a long time for a case to come to a tribunal and in the meantime individuals can suffer a great deal. In 1997 a firefighter, as the only non-white employee at a fire station, was taunted and 'sent to Coventry' by his colleagues. He finally won his complaint of racial discrimination, after years of racial abuse. Colleagues continually mocked him by calling him 'Gunga Din', after the character in a Rudyard Kipling poem, and he was referred to as the "char-wallah". The ordeal shattered his self-confidence.

Question

Do you think verbal racial abuse is just another form of good-natured humour and that some people just make too much fuss, or do you think it's more serious than that?

Question

If quota systems are not the right way to ensure equality in the job market, are there other ways of achieving equality?

RACISM IN IMAGES AND WORDS

For many years the only way in which black people appeared in Hollywood films was as servants - house cleaners, cooks, gardeners - or in other humble forms of employment. They were never shown as important, powerful or clever people. Nor were they shown as having an individual personality.

The Chinese - in fact most people from Asia - were also only seen in certain stereotypical roles. They were portrayed as untrustworthy, cruel, pathetically over-polite, or associated with opium dens. In these ways certain ethnic groups come to be seen only in crude caricature, like cartoon characters. Their existence as real people with real lives and real feelings and thoughts becomes invisible.

The cinema has been a hugely popular medium of entertainment, and images presented in film can influence very large numbers of people.

Black film directors such as Spike Lee are beginning to change the influence of racism in the film industry.

In the United States the stereotypes of black people have changed but often still remain stereotypes. Nowadays you don't see the old 'Southern' image of the black female cook, for example, but you do see the stereotype of the black male criminal. Many black actors, producers and film directors are increasingly aware of this and are improving matters by pushing for appropriate images of black people in films and on TV. Some of the all-black TV soaps, for example, do a lot to present a more varied, normal range of black characters, not just the old stereotypes. The Cosby Show in the USA not only countered racial stereotypes, it also succeeded in gaining an audience of viewers that was larger than almost all other TV shows. Black film directors, such as Spike Lee, often fight hard in their films to tackle the issue of racism directly.

Question

Think about a recent film you have seen featuring black people and white people. Do you think the characters portrayed racial stereotypes?

Find out!

When did films start to introduce black heroes into their stories? Look at a picture-book history of the cinema and see what it tells you about race in films. What conclusions can you draw?

Question

How does what we see on the screen influence how we think about different ethnic groups?

Bill Cosby. Black and ethnic minority celebrities can do a lot to change stereotypes.

THE PRESS

What people read in the newspapers can also influence how they think about other social groups, including ethnic and 'racial' minorities. If, for example, people from India are always presented as poor, starving or the victims of drought, that creates a false picture of Indians in general, even though it is right to report the human tragedies. Newspaper readers may never get to hear about the Indian scientists, writers, entrepreneurs, film-makers, artists, engineers and so on, not to mention the everyday, normal lives of normal people.

Thinking of people from ethnic groups different from your own as 'not real' is part of what allows people to treat others callously and with cruelty: "It doesn't matter. They don't have feelings like we do". That is why anything that paints a picture of any group of people in a certain way can be not just inaccurate but also harmful and dangerous.

Stereotypes in the press may influence and be influenced by stereotypes from other sources. Newspaper journalists who choose to write stories about 'black crime' and who make it into something special instead of looking at the problem of criminal activity through the crime itself, may be reflecting ideas they have received from stereotypes in films, other newspaper articles or elsewhere. They may also be influencing what other writers - film script writers, journalists, novelists, - come to write. In that way stereotypes keep going around and tend not to disappear until people make a conscious effort to tell a different story.

Find out!
How do different newspapers tackle stories about racial issues?

Question
Do you think that people really are influenced by what they read in the papers?

Question
Think of the images of three ethnic groups, including your own. Did any of these images come from films or TV?

Find out!
Find out about the Press Complaints Commission.

ONLY JOKING

Another way in which racism is reinforced is through racist jokes. Most people who enjoy racist jokes think that jokes are not important. They are 'just jokes'. But many jokes depend on stereotypes. Racist jokes depend very much on racist stereotypes and reinforce them. They also hurt. They certainly hurt people they are about. They can also spoil the social environment in which we all live, and so hurt all of us in one way or another.

Question
The English make jokes about the Irish - particularly the southern, Catholic Irish. Is this racism? religious prejudice? just 'a laugh'?

Jokes also spread very quickly. If you hear a joke you know that it has already been on quite a journey from person to person. The fact that it is repeated suggests it is backed up by the community that you belong to. So the racist element becomes 'normalised' and accepted.

Question
Are racist jokes the same or worse than jokes about (a) people with disabilities, (b) mothers-in-law (c) fat people?

Find out!
Where do racist jokes come from? Do any come from professional comedians?

Question
Do you think racist jokes are harmful or harmless? Talk to your friends to see if the answers differ between people from an ethnic minority and those from the majority ethnic group in your school.

FIGHTING RACISM

Whatever governments do or fail to do, in the end it is the responsibility of all of us to make our views known and to challenge racism whenever we encounter it. There are many brave examples from the past of people who have spoken out against racism - many heroes of anti-racist struggles. Some of the best known in recent times have been Nelson Mandela, for his resistance to apartheid in South Africa, and Martin Luther King who was assassinated by a white gunman on April 4th 1968 while he was organising a huge non-violent 'Poor People's March' on Washington, uniting poor whites, African Americans, native Americans ('Indians'), Latinos and many other groups.

Find out!

When did Martin Luther King deliver his 'I have a dream' speech and what did he say in it?

After Dr King's non-violent approach seemed to have failed in the United States, other forms of resistance to racism were developed. Some of the leaders of these movements, such as Malcolm X, also became famous.

Martin Luther King has become a symbol of peaceful but powerful resistance to racism.

A CHANGING WORLD...

Nowadays all over the world people are discovering that it isn't necessarily impossible or even very difficult for people of different ethnic groups to live, learn, work and play together. Mass communication is shrinking the world, bringing people closer together, making differences in ethnicity and physical form - skin colour, facial shape, hair type - seem normal and unremarkable. More and more people are enjoying friendships across differences and many people's lives, especially in big modern cities, mix features of many different cultures in music, clothes, fashion, food, forms of entertainment, even in ways of talking! Racism may have begun a long way back in history but modern life could make it a thing of the past.

Many battles remain to be fought. Unemployment, poor job prospects and bad schooling should not fall disproportionately on any ethnic group, and where it does, racism needs to be addressed. And while the civil rights legislation of the 50s and 60s in the United States removed one legal framework of racism, how laws are applied and used, and how policing is carried out in every country still needs to be monitored for racism. And sadly there are always those who even today try to stir up racial hatred

Where governments and schools take a lead, people often spontaneously find the will to work happily together.

and fear of people who are ethnically different. All these and other forms of racism have to be fought. However, there are strong signs that the modern world can leave racism behind as a thing of the past if it has the will to do so.

In Everyday Life

Racism is both suffered and fought by people every day in very ordinary situations. All of us can speak out against racist behaviour when we see it happening - whether or not we are on the receiving end of it. When we hear racist jokes, when we find that we or our friends are being treated differently because

of 'race' or ethnicity, when we see a piece of journalism in the newspaper that we think perpetuates some ethnic stereotype, we can make our views known. Even such apparently small ways can help to fight racism.

We can also become better informed about racism and its effects. There are many organisations world-wide that inform people about racism and anti-racist struggles. We can write to some of these. Some are listed at the end of this book.

Tackling racism today is the way to ensure harmony for future generations.

FURTHER READING

Listed below are a range of books about racism. Some are available from good bookshops. They should all be available through a good public library.

Causes and Consequences of the African - American Civil Rights Movement, M. Weber, Evans Brothers Ltd 1997

Causes and Consequences of the End of Apartheid, C. Bradley, Evans Brothers Ltd 1995

Causes and Consequences of Independence in Africa, Dr. K Shillington, Evans Brothers Ltd 1997

History in Writing; Slavery, Christine Hatt, Evans Brothers Ltd 1997

The Holocaust - a guide for teachers and students, The Holocaust Educational Trust, 1995

From Prejudice to Genocide - Learning About the Holocaust, Carrie Supple, Trentham Books

When hate comes to town: community responses to racism and fascism, Searchlight Community Handbook, Searchlight Educational Trust, 37B New Cavendish Street, London W1M 8JR

Refugees - We Left Because We Had To - An Educational Book for 14 - 18 year olds, Jill Rutter, The Refugee Council, 3 Bondway, London SW8 1SJ

Daily Racism: The Press and Black People in Britain, P. Gordon and A. Newnham, Runnymeade Trust 1989

Different Worlds: Racism and Discrimination in Britain, P. Gordon and A. Newnham, Runnymeade Trust 1986

Routes of Racism Video (VHS) (about Racism and young people in the London Borough of Greenwich), 28 mins, with manual for teachers and youth workers, International Centre for Intercultural Studies, Institute of Education, University of London, 20 Bedford Way, London WC1H OAL

Black Women in Britain, J. Harriot B.T. Batsford Ltd. 1992

Racism (Let's Talk About), A. Grinsell, Wayland 1995

Racism (Points of View), Y. Alitshai and C. Brown, Wayland 1991

Challenging Racism (Issues for the Nineties), C. Donnellan, Independence 1989

How Racist Are We? (Issues for the 90s), C. Donnellan, Independence 1993

Racism, P. Sanders and S. Myers Gloucester Press, 1995

The Black and White Media Book: A handbook for the study of racism, J. Twitchin, Trentham Books 1998

Brandon Centre of Counselling and Psycotherapy for Young People
26 Prince Of Wales Road
London NW5
Tel: 0171 267 4792
Provides advice and counselling for young people on a wide range of issues.

British Refugee Council
3 Bondway
London SW8
Tel: 0171 582 6922
Provide the services of Education Advisors who provide teaching materials that explore the issues of racism and arrange visits to schools to discuss these issues. They also work closely with refugee children who have had to flee their countries without their parents.

Commission for Racial Equality
Elliot House
10 -12 Allington Street
London SW1 5EH
Tel: 0171 828 7022
Provides the services of youth officers to give support and information to teenagers who are suffering from racism. They hold information on specialist organisations nationwide and can provide resources for teachers and youth workers.

Alternatively, you can contact your local **Racial Equality Council**. Telephone numbers are available from the Commission for Racial Equality, or from your local phone book. They provide support and information as well as putting you in touch with specialised organisations in your area.

Central Scotland Racial Equality Council
Rooms 8 & 9
Park Street Annexe (West)
Falkirk FK1 1RE
Tel: 01324 610950

Commission for Racial Equality
Pearl Assurance House
14th Floor
Gray Friars Road
Cardiff CF1 3AG
Tel: 01222 388977

Commission for Racial Equality in Northern Ireland
Scottish Legal House
65 - 67 Chichester Street
Belfast BT1 4JT
Tel: 01232 315996

Childline
Freepost 1111
London N10 BR
Tel: 0800 1111
24-hour helpline for children and young people

Migrants Resource Centre
24 Churton Street
London SW1
Tel: 0171 834 6650
Offers support and advice to recent migrants, both adults and children, on issues such as housing, schooling and benefits.

National Children's Bureau
8 Wakely Street
London E1V 7QE
Tel: 0171 843 6000
Provides information on where to get help on a wide range of issues, especially for those who work in child care.

Runnymeade Trust
133 Aldersgate Street
London EC1A 4JA
Provides information on the services available to young people experiencing racism.

**Equal Opportunity
Commission**
380 Lonsdale Street
Melbourne Vic 3000
Tel: (03) 9281 7111

**Equal Opportunity
Commission**
Westralia Square
141 St Georges Terrace
Perth W.A 6000
Tel: (08) 9264 1930

Equal Opportunity Board
Level 11/28 Margaret Street
Sydney N.S.W. 2000
Tel: (02) 9248 3555

**Commonwealth Dept. of
Immigration and
Multicultural Affairs**
2 Lonsdale Street
Melbourne Vic 3000
Tel: 131881

**Commonwealth Dept. of
Immigration and
Multicultural Affairs**
Level 22, 477 Pitt Street
Sydney N.S.W 2000
Tel: 131881

**Commonwealth Dept. of
Immigration and
Multicultural Affairs**
216 St Georges Terrace
Perth W.A. 6000
Tel: 131881

**Commonwealth Dept. of
Immigration and
Multicultural Affairs**
313 Adelaide Street
Brisbane QLD 4000
Tel: 131881

INDEX